Not Everything Thrown Starts a Revolution

Not Everything Thrown Starts a Revolution

Stephen S. Mills

SIBLING RIVALRY PRESS

LITTLE ROCK / ARKANSAS │ DISTURB / ENRAPTURE

Sibling Rivalry Press, LLC
PO Box 26147
Little Rock, AR 72221
info@siblingrivalrypress.com
www.siblingrivalrypress.com

ISBN: 978-1-943977-52-9
Library of Congress Control No. 2018941801

This title is housed permanently in the Rare Books and Special Collections Vault of the Library of Congress.

First Sibling Rivalry Press Edition, September 2018

For anyone who has ever believed too much

Table of Contents

Part II: New York, Present Day

Preface

How quickly we fall

      victim

to our own belief systems.

How one voice echoing

      finds us

sitting still in our car
when we still had a car

      radio on

listening.

Part I:
New England
Early-18th Century

Part I:
New England
Early-18th Century

"The perpetrators of suicide by proxy committed murder with the intention of bringing about their own death by execution and thus avoiding eternal damnation that befell direct suicides,"

– Professor Kathy Stuart

18th Century Melancholia

"The problem with the past is everyone remembers it differently,"

– Julie Marie Wade

Stories like this one often begin with obligations
      and duties and expectations,
and with what we think we know of the past and the present—
      unable to see the future.

And so she moves through space, our heroine,
      (if that's the right word for her)
from one spot to another,
from one home to another,
from one man to another
      (as some of us are known to do).

But nothing truly terrible is going to happen to her—
      nothing horrific will set this story into motion—
and I know this might surprise you,
or upset you,
or maybe you will question what I mean by the words

      truly and *terrible* and *happen*

or maybe you will think I'm *just being a man*
      (something a wife on a network sitcom might say).

And it's fair to question me,
this narrative,
these facts (if there are any),
but this isn't about cruel husbands,
or brutal fathers,

or lusty preachers
        (how boring would that be?).

No, this is about what people used to call *an excess of black bile*
        (I'm not making that up).
Yes, this story is about black bile and numbness
        and a quiet sadness that swallows logic
and an all-too-familiar fascination
        with everything stopping—
every single thing.

16 Miles

Her mother said, *It's not so far.*
But mothers lie in stories like these.

Pa made no promises like necklaces
in pockets that never stay put.

She'd never been more than a mile
or two from home (which sounds stranger
than it is—time period and all),

but never more than a mile or two
from the sound of the chickens,
or mother's cooking, or brother's teasing.

She told Harold (her soon-to-be husband)
all of this in a letter—pen shaky.

He wrote back in sharp slants: letters
pushing into each other, nearing the end
of the page, ready to jump.

Not so far—but mothers lie,
and papas stay quiet,
and brothers find others to tease.

It was almost summer. She was almost
seventeen (or if you are into musicals:
sixteen going on seventeen).

How She Became a Disappointed Wife

It started in a field (like any field)
on a summer day (like any summer day).

And she (Mary Agnes—our heroine)
was still young, still beautiful. Hair bright red.

And she held a hat: white, yellow ribbon.
Her hair whipped behind. She didn't mind

air in her hair. The pull backward into green.
And there was a man (there's always a man).

A husband (Harold). A worn face. A wrinkled brow.
A quilted blanket beneath. One his mother made.

Long ago. Dead now. Gone. A woman
she won't become (wives are not mothers).

They don't speak. But eyes move the wide
expanse of land. No one in sight (or is that just

a trick of the eye?). Unsure, his hand moves
in quick jerks. Touches her back.

The fabric of her dress: soft in rough hands.
She turns (surprised). He moves hand to face.

His hand. Her face. So near him.
His throat dry. He swallows. Lips move to neck.

Her neck. A brief kiss. A blush on cheeks.
His cheeks. Eyes cast down. His eyes

(embarrassed). Hands fail to sides (not fall).
The hot wind rushes forward. Her hair moving

like the grass swallowing them up. It's over now.
Man and wife. Small. Insignificant.

Harold Watches Mary Agnes

From the doorway, back to him, the red of her hair
      bright in firelight. Her hands working dough.
Beating the life into it (or is it out of it?).
      He knows nothing of baking bread.
He stays silent. Words rarely form—throat always dry.
      Not used to being a husband. Used up
by the land. An old fool. But she—young—moves
      soft on her feet. Her skin flushed with heat—
everything glowing (or is that just his imagination?).

There was that day in the field their first year together
      when he touched her like a man should—
a husband should. When he kissed her neck
      and made her smile. He smiled back, then blushed,
then turned away. An old man. Rough hands.
      And at night when he moves inside her
(as husbands are known to do), she tightens against him,
      turns from his face, his wrinkled brow,
his sunken eyes. She doesn't desire him (can we blame her?).
      She holds breath against thrusts. So clumsy.
He rolls away. They do not speak.

John Plymouth (a Neighbor) Commits Suicide, Mary Agnes Imagines

His body free of breath on the cottage floor.
His nails full of earth.

A body that once worked the land,
fed chickens, milked cows, cared for a quiet
woman—a simple woman—a simple man.

And how the air must have left him.
How he stopped.
How his hands no longer worked
the wood of trees into tables and chairs,
like the ones Harold bought
that fill this very room.

I imagine the steel entering his flesh.
Is human skin like animal?
Potato? Carrot?
Like making stew?
Chopping bits into a pot
in this home with this table and chairs
made by a dead man's hands?
A man we are meant to forget.

I imagine quite a bit of blood on the floor
with the body no longer moving.
The blood inching along, filling cracks.

And the rush to her heart when she found him:
her hands quick to the body.

The sight of it all.
Her own body suddenly as free
as his from breath.
No husband left.

Reverend White denied him a proper burial.
The greatest of sins, they say.
So they dumped him in the river
through a hole in the bottom
of the wagon so his soul
could not escape,
could not wreak havoc on the land
causing disasters, hail storms, withered crops.

Superstitions are alive and well.

Now I imagine his body floating,
almost dancing through the riverbed,
nibbled by fish,
denied the grace of God.
For he left this world by choice.
By his own hand.
A hand that once took knife to bark.

It is almost enough to shake
the melancholy from my bones.

The Village Burns John Plymouth's Woodwork

a superstition
a ritual
a warding off of evil

a crowd gathers
cheers
throws chairs
table legs
scraps of wood
into flame
in the center
of the village
where John's work burns

bright light
in night sky
village center
blazing hot on skin
glowing orange
then red
then dark

repeat

wood succumbing
to the heat
the weight
the desire

burning

against skin
against faces
against the bright light
spreading over mouths
of the crowd
in the center
of the village
of the people
of Mary Agnes

of those who once
sang the praises
of a simple man
and his simple knife

The Village Boys Play in the Ash

Black hands on white skin. The mark of death—
destruction—a man's work (John's work).

But child's play now. Boys chase each other
shouting in morning air. Heavy with smoke.

  The cleanest boy will win.

Obadiah is quick on his feet. Small and able.
His hair the color of wheat suddenly streaked

with black. A boy at his back. A fist full of ash.
He'll get his revenge (he's patient for being so young).

The other boys have tackled the pudgiest one
to the ground. He didn't stand a chance (did he?).

He's down in the black—white skin slipping away.
Hand after hand of ash. Ending his chance of winning.

Obadiah waits. Watches. Fists full. Then one swift
move and his hands take flight—rain down on the two

closest boys. They turn—quick, but Obadiah is ready
with pockets of more. Now it is black ash to pink lips.

The boys before him flash the white of their teeth.

Execution Sunday

Body to body they sit (the living).
Packed church.
Reverend White weaves
a tale of redemption:
a lost soul
(a cinematic journey).

The convicted—a man—
sits front pew: a body at peace.
God forgiven (or so they say).

When we lose Christ, we lose our way.

Thieving by night.
A body awake—a surprise.
He killed her—knife in stomach
(without even thinking).
An old woman too.
So much blood, they say,
when knife meets middle.

Mary Agnes reads the broadsheet
from the boy on the corner:
the convict's biography,
sketches of the murder scene,
his confession.

And now here the execution sermon:
the lesson learned (all neat and tidy).

Reverend White is all fire
and brimstone and warnings
from the pulpit:

> *If this man can walk into the gates of heaven,*
> *why can't you? Repent today. Save your soul.*

And then they walk
body to body
to the center of the village:
the execution site.
Forgiveness and death by hanging.
Just another Sunday morning.

> *Amen.*

The Doctor Speaks of Mary Agnes' Melancholia

(In a patronizing-know-it-all voice)

Time outdoors will do her good—fresh air, sunshine,
walks among flowers, trees, God's creatures.
Maybe along the river where everything is greener.
Where the children play, swim, splash.
She will see the light again. Smile again. Maybe time
with other women too. Church groups.
Have her sing in the choir. Lovely voice, I'm sure.

Praise be to God.

Diet too. A buildup probably. Black bile, they say.
Let it out. Water. Bread. Nothing too complex.
A week or two and everything should be better.
Us men, Harold, don't feel sad the same way
as women folk do. They are gentler, softer, more delicate.
Like a child. Like a little dove learning to fly.
She just needs to find a bit of air. Fill her lungs deep.
Breathe in and out. She'll be just fine.
Her old self again in no time. Fresh air. A good man.
Patience. Maybe a child soon. God willing.

Fragments from Mary Agnes' Diary

Days are full of heat. This bread flat. Not like Mother taught. Nothing is said. Has my hair lost its light? Darker than before.

❧

These women bore me. Harold says sing in the choir. Harold says have a baby if you want. Harold says bake more bread. Harold says go for walks. Harold says…

But no child will take root here. Be sure of that.

❧

There is darkness in this land—even when it's bright. It creeps in. It longs to swallow me whole. I see it everywhere.

❧

Last night I swear I saw a ghost. Was it John? Back from the dead? His knife in his hand? I swear he was sitting at our table. The one he made. The chair he made. He wouldn't look at me no matter how loud I called.

But I kept calling. Howling. Begging.

Then I woke.

❧

I want to cut my hair short. Free myself from it. Can you imagine what people would say? A woman with short red hair.

∽

Children run fast. Swim. Splash. Age has not taught them fear. But I fear for them. Time will catch them. Mark them. The beast is waiting. It is always waiting.

∽

I cannot stop thinking of bodies that do not move. I read the broadsheets from the vile man on the corner. Some made up I'm sure. Death. Murder. Executions. Harold never notices the missing pennies or the papers folded in my drawer under the linens.

∽

Doctors know nothing of women. Probably little of men. Fresh air. Lungs deep. Puts me to sleep. Does God know much more? Will he save me? I pray every day. It's all I have.

∽

Days go on and on and on and Harold is always the same. Nothing bothers that man. Peace. He's at peace. I envy that at times. Fear it others.

34

Mary Agnes Dreams of Execution

The boards creak beneath my feet—bare.
Hands at sides—soft.
A breeze in my hair: red blowing behind.

The crowd is stunned by my poise,
my grace,
my confidence
in facing my execution.

The hangman's hands are firm.
He casts a shadow deep and wide.
There's comfort in his darkness.

His hands move white linen over head.
A hood. Next comes rope
at my neck.
The one Harold kissed
our first summer: just once.

Reverend White leads everyone in prayer.
Salvation promised.
I shall be free.

The noose tightens.
The crowd says, *Amen*.
They fall silent watching my body,
my red hair,
my hands not trembling.

Then the boards beneath me give way.
Down I go.
Feet dangling,
twitching,
eventually stopping.

The crowd cheering,
sobbing,
buying souvenirs
with my name etched on them:
Mary Agnes Hanged for Murder.

Mary Agnes Watches Obadiah

(and you know where this is going—
        don't you?)

a woman's eye / a boy's body

how quick he moves
so easy   with his limbs
which will only grow stronger

and she—a woman
uncomfortable in her skin
in her movement

she watches / he splashes
other boys all around

how free children are
when no adult is present

        He'll do just fine.
        He'll be just fine.

innocence hangs on him
like a fresh coat of snow
he will not tarnish
she's sure of that

Obadiah Asks His Mother About Salvation

(In a genuine and caring voice)

All children are innocent, Obadiah.
Especially you.
For you will grow strong and bold
and handsome.
Hands bigger than mine soon enough.
Taller too.
Legs longer.
But innocence, Obadiah, has a way
of growing thin with age.
We need God more with years in our bones.
But days like today when the sun is hot
and the water still cool,
it's hard for any of us to not feel
the salvation promised.
But boys grow into men,
and men easily turn hard.
So remember softness,
the smell of the spring flowers,
your mother's kiss,
your friends' laughter—
remember this moment.
This innocence.
For it won't last forever.

The Drowning / The Confession

It was quick—he was quick—almost too quick.

/ I drowned the boy. It was me.

A stone to slow him down. He stopped to look around.

/ I caught him. Hand over mouth. He wanted to scream.

I wanted to scream back.

/ I killed the boy. Obadiah, they called him.

I held him tight to my chest like his mother might.

/ I used Harold's knife thrown in the bushes. Find it.

I told the boy it'd be okay. There was a plan. God's plan. Mine.

/ I sliced at him hard. Catching more air than skin.

A bit of blood came down his face. Nowhere near his throat.

/ I aimed for the tender part. The white of his neck.

He rubbed his wound. Only a thin line of red. A scratch.

/ I shoved him hard. Had to finish what I started.

The roar of the river filled ears. His. Mine.

/ I leapt in too. Held him down. A trickle of pink.

He fought. His head bloody. His lungs filling. My arms aching.

/ I couldn't stop. I sang to him. I prayed.

God doesn't punish children. Heaven will be his—ours.

/ I waited until he stopped moving.

No more thrusts. No more power left is his limbs. Or mine.

/ I am here to confess.

A Bloody Defense: A Lawyer Speaks

It's in the blood—
        in the place—the space—the what do they say?
The crevice—the spot—the between the legs

of a woman.

Monthly cleansing but risky
        for *wicked comes this way:*
bloody, dark, and brooding: black bile.

A defensible claim.

One cannot be responsible for evil acts
when blood is trickling down—down—down.

Check her rags.
Check her legs.
Check the color of her stains.

Build a defense.

No evil intent is proven
when menstrual blood is present.
A claim to insanity.
A chance to spare a life.

An unfortunate accident? Yes.
A child gone too soon? Yes.
But to heaven, remember.

Quite defensible if blood is found.

Check her rags.
Check her legs.
Check the color of her stains.

It's all quite defensible if—if—if—

How Does a Mother Respond?

Does she fall to the ground
fists beating dirt?

Does she scream like a wild
animal caught in a trap?
A howl—maybe?
A deep guttural utterance?

(Is she Meryl Streep
or Shirley MacLaine
or maybe Sally Field?)

Does she turn to God
or away from God?

Does she strike fear
in those around her?
Curse them?
Make them think she
might be just as evil?
The cause of it all?

Does she place blame
in all the wrong places?
Or all the right ones?

Does she become stoic?
A model citizen?

A model Christian?
A model woman?

Does she forgive?
Does she pray?
Does she move on?

Or does she understand
the longing to escape?
The thrill of loose
hair in wind?

Harold Visits Mary Agnes in Prison

The cell is darker—damper—colder than husbands expect.

She doesn't look up.
He doesn't find words.

Only eyes that search for the fire in her—
flickering
gone
(was it his imagination?).

Hands busy in her lap.
Folding her prison dress
(if that's the right word)
over and over.
Constant motion
as if he's not there.

And still
his words do not come.
Do not form.
Throat dry.
Not even in his brain does he know what to say.

What words can fix this deed?

A child dead.
His wife confessed.
No defense.
An execution set.

Reverend White Ponders a Manipulation

of texts—words—teachings.

Questions the mind that can swim
in circles never finding solid ground.

A woman fearing her own sins might find
ways around—but could she? Would she?

Could she really think the impossible—
do the impossible? A child's death?

No. Not a woman. Not a Christian woman.
Not this woman known to me.

But pieces fall into minds—fragments.
Teachings get boggled—mixed inside.

Sin and forgiveness. But punishment too.
I've been so clear—have I not?

But then the unthinkable. Am I the fool?
Or she? Or maybe both?

The devil is near.
No, the devil is here.

She Doesn't Look: The Village Speaks

not at all
doesn't look
like a monster might
a murderer
a child killer

but her eyes maybe
her hands always moving
her smile less than pleasing
maybe she does look
a little like
a little like they say

but she doesn't look
doesn't look
like a woman with a plan
like a wicked woman
wicked comes this way

that hair though
red
shocks the light
the night
looks like monsters might

maybe she does
look a little like
a little like
they say she might
but violent

she doesn't look
look no
not violent no

but maybe they say
or she says
or she looks
I guess
maybe yes
a little like
what they say she might

And Then She Hangs

a woman
a spectacle
red hair
in black
color of mourning
for years spent
inside
the space of a home
a town
a place
she never chose
16 miles

and the wind is light
but hot
spring gone
summer again
children laughing
near the river bend

the crowd
in the center
of the village
bigger
louder
in higher spirits

a man
brown coat
sells etchings

of her face
and pamphlets
that catch flight
land at feet

she is everything
she needs to be:
a murderess
forgiven by God
forced to pay
the ultimate price

a lesson
in her skin
in her sorrow
in her act
but she knows
truth lacks
in this space
between her
and the crowd
between her
and her husband's face
of disbelief

there is power
here
in keeping quiet
in accepting
created fate

and there is time
more than you think
between
the floorboards
and the earth

a space only she
can know
pausing perfectly
between
life and death
right and wrong
dark and light
(or is it light and dark?)
where freedom wakes
and she
takes flight

Part II:
New York
Present Day

"So this is who we are, the jailers, the jailed.
This is the spirit of our age,"

– C.D. Wright

"The choice may have been mistaken, / the choosing was not,"

– Dot in *Sunday in the Park with George*

21st Century Melancholia

The nanny on the subway wants everyone to know the baby isn't hers—not hers—she's the nanny—not a mother. Even if the baby looks a lot like her, he's not. *Not mine*, she repeats over and over as she laughs nervously into the train car as an older Hispanic woman makes faces at the baby and says again how much he looks like the blonde-haired nanny. Across the car, a woman reads a book about unionizing sex workers. It lays open to a chapter called "My Ass is My Own." She doesn't make faces at the baby. A handsome man sits down near the stroller—smiles at the baby—makes eyes at the nanny. She repeats without prompting, *he isn't mine.* In the center of the car, three young women hold two giant silver balloons in the shapes of a 2 and a 4. Someone's birthday, I suppose. Someone's 24 or is it 42? I want to tell them the next decade is full of disappointments and confusions and fuck-ups. Because what decade isn't? And when the train stops and the birthday women begin to exit, one accidentally lets go of the number 2. It floats to the top of the car bobbing there—hovering over us like a cloud or a drone or a sparkly bird—an airplane. The baby looks up and squeals with delight. The nanny forgets her denial of the baby and watches in amazement as the girls struggle to recapture the balloon—for no one they know is turning 4. And the man next to the nanny remembers letting go of a balloon himself in the park when he was seven and didn't have a nanny or any way to recapture the balloon swallowed by the sky. And the sex worker smiles too as her book slips from her lap and flops closed on the sticky floor below. We all stop—mesmerized by our own reflection staring back at us in distorted neoprene.

Land Is Something You Crave or You Don't

"And God said let there be light, and there was light.
And God said let there be corn, and there was Indiana."

—Bruce Snider

Soil under fingernails, wiped onto pants,
smeared across shoes, laces like earthworms—
what does it mean to crave the land?

To dig with bare hands into earth
that will one day swallow us whole—
or maybe not? You want your body

donated to science—sliced and used
for a greater purpose—me? I'm not so sure,
but the idea of ashes in the air

has always seemed beautiful.
Something about spreading yourself thin,
not knowing where you might land,

but even then you end up in the ground
somewhere—trapped—don't you?
Just probably not where you started.

We started in Indiana where land locks you tight,
and corn stalks nick your skin,
and blood beads along your arms,

your bare legs, your sandaled feet.
They say all land is blood soaked,
but is it all craved? Did I ever long for it?

The loneliness of open spaces?
Looking out, seeing no one, nothing—
empty for miles? But that's just a trick

of the eye. We can't see everything
that lives and dies before us:
a survival mechanism.

I spent my childhood planting seeds,
picking weeds, then vegetables:
food we put on the table to help us grow

strong Midwestern bodies.
But I've traded fields for buildings,
for concrete, for the rattling of the radiator

in my New York apartment.
For tight spaces. For bodies stacked
on top of each other. Bodies that lock

you in. Keep you from falling down
on the subway, the escalator, the sidewalk.
It is here that land becomes mysterious again.

How We Became Sluts

It seems like something that would begin in the body—
    a fleshy kind of desire,
    an impulse,
    something hard to control like hunger.

But it began in the mind—mine—yours—
    where ideas fester,

    expand,

    become our existence.

                               ∽

I might regret the first time,
if I let myself regret such things—
such actions—such desires.

But I fucked him to prove I could.
It was dark. His house full
of shadows. He got on all fours.

Me behind. The condom so tight—
not used to wearing them.
He came quickly. It was done.

You read *The Ethical Slut*, which is mostly
common sense to us now and some bullshit too.
It's a little late for a manual after so many
years of doing it on our own.

The book talks of crushes—how they happen
in the openness, but how they pass us by—
leave us. Maybe that's why they're called crushes:
they break down—crumble easily.

We are good at talking—
you and I—probably too much
sometimes. But words
are our currency—our lifeline.

It's 75 degrees in New York
as he rams his cock down my throat
making me feel used in the best way possible.

I've never sucked cock in a park before.
In public? Yes, but not a park.
There's dirt and broken glass below us.

I aim knees carefully, trying not to care.
Another man watches—cock out.
There is danger in this—or could be

or should be—stories we tell to scare
ourselves out of desire: what if
he's a murderer rapist? Too late.

When he cums, it explodes all over
my face, my tank top, my own cock.
I remove my underwear to clean myself up—

unprepared for a cruise in the park.
Then I slip them inside my *New Yorker* tote
(free with subscription).

We part ways at the top of the path.
I snap his picture from the back
with my phone and send it to you.

On the subway platform, an elderly
European couple asks for directions.
I help them. My hairband is lost in the dirt.

My red hair loose—longer than
it's ever been. On the train home,
a man reads a newspaper. Headline:

Death Penalty Given in Boston Marathon Bombing.

～∞～

Sometimes I chat with other guys in other cities—
other states—sometimes other countries
and weave wild stories to make them cum.

We trade pictures. I tell lies. I try to figure
out what they want. What they desire.
What they are afraid to tell their lovers.

～∞～

My doctor says I have the clap.
Tells me if I remember (or if I am in contact with)
my sexual partners, I should tell them.
Some I know.
Others I don't.
Like the tall thick man with dreads
who sucked both our cocks
at the bathhouse party during Pride Weekend.
I send some texts.
I take some pills.
I wait seven days.
You clap your hands when you see me.

～∞～

While you work evenings, I binge
watch *The Americans* imagining us
as spies using our bodies to get

information for our country
while trying to navigate a real
marriage—real responsibilities.
For we are married now.
Not just in name, but in real hard law:
paper trails and rings and photographs.

Do we appear as something we are not?
Commies as Americans? Kind white
married folk but really sex maniacs?
I feel like a spy trying to find the *right*
information for the *right* cause
but then wondering if it's all worth it
in the end. It's not easy going against
the masses. Keri Russell's hair understands.

∞

Years ago, I kept a list
thinking it would be easy to track
the bodies.
But then there were bars
and parties and cruises—
hands and mouths and holes
hard to keep track of.
The list faded.
Bodies I don't remember anymore.

Then the ones I do:
the college boy with the Peter Pan tattoo,

the white boy in the cowboy boots
who was bad in bed,
the cute choir boy with the loose hole,
the black muscle bottom who kissed his own biceps
while I fucked him and tried not to laugh.

So many bodies that come
and go through the years—
stories we forget to write down—
lost in the mattress.

∽

As a teenager of the 1990s,
I spent late nights in AOL chat rooms
talking with 40-something divorcées.
I wove tales of bad husbands
and the struggles of middle-aged dating.
Found ways to comfort the lonely—
the glow of the screen lighting my smile—
amazed at all I could get away with.

∽

Some nights our bodies move together
like the first years—like time might be running
backward—a hunger—a thirst.
Something to shake the melancholy from my bones.

⸎

It was a finger that inched forward—
then a hand fully clasped—fingers interlaced.
Then a kiss. A blush. We were just boys.

And then there were nights tangled
in each other's bodies and in that quilt
your grandmother made,
which years had turned to rags.

I feared I might wake to your neck
noosed in its shreds—a body so still
next to mine still breathing.

⸎

We take pills now to prevent HIV infection—
like out of some gay boy sci-fi flick:
blue on tongues. We laugh at the freedom
from fear. We talk of bodies we want—
old times together—of changing landscapes.

We speak of anything and everything and nothing.
And tomorrow I will text you pictures
of me fucking a guy we met once. My dick bare
in his ass. You will send me a smiley face—
or maybe a simple: *I love you.*

My Husband Talks of Floating

It's called a floater: a body in the water.
Doesn't matter how it got there: fell, jumped,
pushed. It's still a floater. A body taking on water.

Breaking down. Becoming something else entirely.
But the name also implies that one will
eventually find it there on the surface bobbing.

That it will be saved from the hardships
of the unknown. From families left to guess.
To wonder *what if*.

It's your job to call the time of death,
which seems silly since it's not the actual time
of death, but the time it was found.

Actually, it's not even that since you are not the one
to pull the floater from the Hudson. The time
of death is the time on your watch

when you unzip the body bag, look it in the face,
and call it dead. It is your duty. The police
and search crew do not have the authority

to say what is dead and what is alive.
But you do. Such power when you think about it.
But when does a floater become a body

again? A person? Today was your first
and now over dinner—some Italian place—
you speak of it in facts and short descriptions.

How the skin looked pale but intact,
how she was missing her pants,
but still had her eyes.

Answers to questions I didn't know to ask.
But then you say part of her nose was gone.
And I wonder what that means exactly.

Where did it go? Eaten by fish? Rubbed away
by the power of water? For water
is more powerful than we ever want to admit.

And then I think of me as a kid
on my back in the swimming pool
doing the "dead man's float."

My ears clogged with water, my eyes open
to the silent world above. Just floating there
hoping to be spotted. To be rescued.

To be called back to life.

Self-Portrait as a Glass Thrown Against a Wall

like glitter when it hits
when it sticks
when it sprinkles the ground
shards and splinters
fragments of a body
moving through a crowd
a dramatic *fuck you*
a privilege you don't get to have
for you are not a white lady on a TV show
and then a bathroom mirror
an image you don't always like
an image you question
How can you be this stupid?
and then there's the shattered glass
you left behind
full of gin and tonic—was it?
or whisky and coke?
not anymore
now a million pieces
but of course that's an exaggeration
there can't really be a million—
can there?

By the Numbers

There have been 1,412 executions since 1976 in the United States. 15 women. 1,397 men. 22 for crimes committed as juveniles. 1,237 died by lethal injection. 158 by electrocution. 11 by gas chamber. 3 by hanging. And 3 more by firing squad. Aim. Shoot. Die. Most have been in the South. Most by state equals Texas at 527. Everything is bigger in Texas where my whole immediate family has relocated. Where my nieces and nephew will grow—mature—identify as Texans. Where I will never feel at home.

∽

There were 12 of us in the cell at central booking like 12 angry men or maybe 12 disciples or maybe a dirty dozen. Many had done this before and were confident about going home after seeing the judge. Others worried over outstanding warrants or perceived weapons found on their persons or pay phones that didn't work—families they couldn't call. 50 cents nobody had. For we had to pay to call anyone. They don't show that on TV. And of the 12 only 3 were white (myself included) and I wondered if I could make a prison family out of this if I had to. One was twisting himself into a ball having a panic attack while calling for a doctor that would never come. The other couldn't even look up from his bloodstained white dress shirt—his expensive black dress shoes—his preppy blond haircut. He would be of no use.

∽

Race by numbers by executions by victims. 55.5% of people put to death have been white. 34.7% black. 8.1% Hispanic. 1.7% other. But it gets trickier—more complicated. You are more likely to be sentenced to death if you murder a white person. 75% of the victims of death row inmates are white even though white people only make up 50% of murder victims. See it's not so simple. Not so easy. Not so colorblind.

⌒

18 hours. I was held for only 18 hours. But long enough to not forget the feel of steel on wrists or the metal of the bench I tried to sleep on—the cold of the cell—the cold of March in New York. And the faces—some young—some old. One man's soft eyes—a single tear perpetually falling down his cheek. *How did he do that?* A slight smile reassuring me. See everyone was kind. *In this together. Fight the system. You'll be okay.* One man offered his last quarters to a young Latino kid who was going to Rikers and wanted to yell at someone on the phone in Spanish. I don't know what he said, but there was someone to blame. I only had myself. Like this was coming all along. Like a speeding bullet you can't stop. You can only take. Hope for the best. A clean exit.

⌒

We sentence people to death by numbers. Life sentence to life sentence. Death or not—still death. We order people to do more time than possible. To serve hundreds of years. To go into the future and serve more time. To reincarnate back into the prison system. To be here perpetually. Never free. Always back. Numbers added to numbers added to numbers. Never stopping. Once in—bound to come back.

⌒

4 rats. 12 stale sandwiches. 3 lazy guards. 1 good cop. 6 bad ones. 3 rooms for meeting with lawyers. All walls covered in scratched graffiti. One kid wanted to add his name to the wall by the broken pay phone: phone literally cut in two and hanging by wires unusable. *This is America?* But he couldn't get his quarter to break the paint. And I wanted to tell him maybe that's a sign. A good sign. But I don't know if I believe in signs.

You Don't Look Violent

Which is a way of classifying the body—
mine—as not dangerous, not threatening

Which is a way to confirm perceptions
of violence
of the male form
of what we think we know

As if to say I am not fully what I am / or appear to be
or could be / or should be / or maybe
just wondering how a body like mine survives this long
waist narrow / height average / shoulders broad
a bit of muscle / a bit of bone / a bit of rib caged left and right

But it's more than appearance
it's sound too
like how the voice that leaves these lips is not violent
not masculine / manly / straight-acting / sounding

And then the way one moves through space
like how wrists bend too much
hands speak too loudly
a walk might sway that a way then that a way
or feet might point outward
not straight ahead
not straight at all

My friend says stereotypes can be shortcuts
she means this as a half joke / half truth
and we laugh

like we laughed that day in the gym
before those teenage boys turned to laugh at me
at my effeminate wave of hands
at my voice
at my non-sexual way of being with my female friend

And how we didn't speak of it right away
but how she wanted to go back
back inside / back to those boys / back in time
how she wanted to say something
do something
to defend my honor
my way of being
a being who is not what people
think of as violent
but soft / non-threatening / just an Other

But stereotypes are often wrong
and anyone can find flight
in their hands / fists / legs

Whole bodies can heave into the air like the crashing
of waves on the shore in Florida
where I lived for seven long years
where I went to the gym with my friend after work and laughed
where mornings hung with such humidity
such defeat
such suffocating heat
that anyone could go mad
anyone could go violent

Our Hero (Question Mark) Faces Suicide (Not His)

Two weeks and my ribs still ache.
Each breath in is a reminder.
The rings around my wrists are nearly gone.
Long-sleeves not required.
I only missed one day of work.
Each day now like it was before—
but then the breath and the rib
and the memory that doesn't shake.
And then a man in front of me says
he wants to kill himself.
That there's a bridge on his way home.
In New York, there's always a bridge.
He wants water to cleanse his sins away.
No one will know why. No one will know
what's taken place in this room except me.
He doesn't know anything about my ribs.
Or that each breath I give him sends pain
through my chest. He doesn't know
that I'm looking for my own water.
That only three people know the cause.
But he wants to die. And it is my job—
in this moment—to stop him.
To tell him life is worth continuing.
That mystery is often worse than fact.

The Trouble with Seeing

The eyes of eyewitnesses are unreliable.

The eye   of the mind   of memory   bends
reshapes   what we see   into what we want   to believe
need to believe   need to remember.

Sometimes we are the villains not the heroes.

∞

Jurors are known to put a lot of weight on eyewitnesses.

How certain we want to be
how right   how righteous.

It was him.
It was she.
This happened.
Then this happened.

But eyes are not facts.

∞

In 25 percent of police lineups,
witnesses pick a filler:
a volunteer—a non-criminal.

∞

I voluntarily meet with the Assistant DA—she is sick. Doesn't want to shake hands. We sit. I read a typed statement. She asks questions. I give up rights by doing this. She makes statements about things that did not happen. Eyewitnesses say this and that. Who? She can't say. Wasn't everyone drunk? A system that puts you at a disadvantage. No one is innocent until proven guilty. No one benefits from taking responsibility. Later she tells my lawyer she doesn't believe me.

I want to tell them both that truth and belief are two separate things.

⌘

In cases involving a weapon,
eyewitnesses are known to suffer
from what they call "weapon focus,"
which means they can,
and often do,
accurately describe the weapon used,
but become useless
in describing anything else
including the person holding the weapon.

⌘

The saying *a picture is worth a thousand words*,
always twists in my mind to mean a picture needs
a thousand words to set it right   in the mind

in the eye.

When you remove your glasses
I become a blur—just a figure moving
through your life

and if I do not speak, I could be anyone—
maybe someone better—maybe someone
less anxious—less self-destructive.

But I, with my near-perfect vision,
can always see you
squinting at me

trying to push the blurs back together again.

Self-Portrait as a Danny Lyon Prison Photograph from 1968 at The Whitney

life in black
and white
as guards watch
a parade of bare
ass by bars
sticks clang against metal
it's a shakedown
it's a mix up
it's a revolving door
it's one mistake
one step
one accident
that leads to another
and another
and another
and then it's bare
ass on parade
for guards in Texas brown
but really a shade of gray
in this photograph
smiles you want to smack away
hands on sticks
that touch metal
that touch skin
I am the law
and on they walk
hosed down
in shower stalls
bunks tossed

then back to cages
one step away
here in this museum
on this wall
watching
like a guard with no stick
no badge
no uniform

Domestic Terror

A woman crouches in the corner of a building
on 22nd Street crying over something lost
or something found or maybe just a rush
of recognition: this is how it all turns out:
these tears on this street in this city
where no one will stop or flinch or judge.
And then later on the subway map there's a sticker
that reads *Rikers is Here* with a red arrow
marking the spot—marking the absence—
marking the 10,000 bodies forgotten.
So close, like everything in New York.
20,000 hands on bars (assuming everyone
has two). It's easier to believe in evil
than in the complexity of the human condition.
And it was just yesterday that you rushed
an old woman hit by a taxi to the hospital
knowing well enough she was going die
(*they all die*, you say). But it is your job
to do what you can, to rush her away
in a charade of control: an act the living go
through. Like the men who pulled the car
off of her, prayed over her, imagined she
was still breathing, still trying to talk—
all before you got there with your skills
and gloves and flashing lights, though none
of that would matter in the long run.
The same day Pfizer blocked the last
of their drugs from being used in lethal injections
and somewhere (not here) bodies felt reprieve.
No one wants the responsibility of the kill—
just the dead body. And sometimes I think
of the thrill of seeing Jude Law's cock

in *The Talented Mr. Ripley* when I was 17
and then a different thrill when Matt Damon
smothers that man at the end proving every thing
creeps toward disaster. Spoiler Alert: We are all monsters.
Public executions were eventually banned
in the United States. Evidence showing no
benefit, so we closed the doors. Locked
it all away, but things locked up are still
there whether we remember them or not.
Recently, I've been writing to gay prisoners
through the Black & Pink organization.
One told me to be careful out there in the real
world. *As silly as this sounds*, he wrote, *I feel
safer in here*. But even in the execution room
there is space for the unexpected: the call
from the governor, the meds gone wrong,
a burnt last meal, a stumbled final phrase,
and then the stopping of a heart that feels
like justice for a split second before it fades
into something darker than a room with a body
not moving anymore. Unlike how I imagine you
in the hospital after a call, always confident,
always calm, always accepting the fate of your days.
And now—right now—the air conditioner
is broken on this subway car and it's 1 AM
and everyone wants to go home. Sweat pools. Runs
down faces. We stare at each other in shared misery.
And then begin to count the stops. The blocks.
The numbers rising. And there on the map
circled in red above my head: *Rikers is Here*.

Colloquy

Was it in a bar? *Yes.*

No problem then.
Last month I got a guy off.
A writer, like you.
A mug in the air.
Won the Pulitzer.

But I haven't won the Pulitzer.
Just a gay award.

No priors? No record? Never anything? *No.*
What kind of glass? *A pedestal, I think. Does it matter?*
What was in it? *Gin, I think. Does it matter?*
What were you thinking? *I wasn't. Does it matter?*

They need a story. You're a writer, right?
They need a reason. They can't just believe
that a reasonable person would throw something into the air.

They obviously haven't watched much TV.

Maybe this is the best we can do: a deal.
They don't like that there's no reason.

Is feeling like the whole world is crashing down not a reason?

No.

Is a tightening of the chest—an urge to explode—
an anxiety so deep—not a reason?

No.

Black bile then?

What? No.
A deal. It's the best we can do.

But will I?

Will you what?

Be okay?

My Jesus Year

You wake me whispering,
Foodtown is burning.
And you don't mean a town of food,
but the grocery store around the corner.
The one we've shopped at plenty of times,
though it's too expensive
and no one can ever help you
find what you're looking for.

You smell of the city mixed with the news
of this burning, which makes me ask questions,
which you don't know the answers to.

And suddenly I'm lost in a wave of grief
for a place I didn't even like,
or maybe it's just the fear of fire
deep in my bones—something prehistoric—
a burning so close by, but not here—
not in this room—not in this apartment
in Harlem with our two dogs.
Always a step away.

∞

New Year's Eve.
Us in Times Square.
You in your uniform.
Me with whisky on my breath.
Us like some post-WWII poster.
And then the countdown.

And the ball sliding
all glitz and lights
like all the years I watched from home:
a kid in Indiana
dreaming of a city I'd never been to,
dreaming of you: a man I didn't know yet,
dreaming of a life that sometimes feels too real now,
and then how the confetti fell
from the sky like giant raindrops—
or was it shrapnel?

∽

By the boarded-up store,
locals bob
in the dumpster
collecting canned goods
thrown away by law
though nothing is wrong with them.
Carts fill with the clang of metal
and glass and then a jar breaks free
and olives flood the sidewalk: slick green.
No one cares.
I smile as more cans pop
over the side into eager hands.
The sky is dimming
into evening.
The air still thick
with burning.

Last week we sat in a theater
and watched Patrick Bateman
wonder (in song) if he's just
a version of the end of days,
standing on the brink of human
destruction—killing to feel
alive—wanting someone to stop
him, but no one will.

And I wonder about my own days,
my own end, my own bend
toward self-destruction: a redheaded
temper or so they used to call it.
Or what of my desire to throw
things against walls? To watch
them shatter? Not everything
thrown starts a revolution.
You should know that.

The woman on the corner
is selling futures for 5 dollars
outside the abandoned coffee shop
on 7th Avenue and 27th Street,
but I want to know
how much the past is.
How much to go backward.

To explain how I got here
on this street corner
on this day
looking at this woman
in her scarf and beads.

But she doesn't have answers
or prices for what has been,
only what will be.
Five dollars will tell me
what's in store: fortune or despair,
but not the missteps
that got me here,
not the story of these thirty-three years.

And there's a garden in this story too,
but far away from here.
Another country.
A bust of her head.
Her own room.
Flowers and herbs.
Old women on benches
and one inside who is eager
to a chat about Virginia,
about the age of the stove,
the pieces in the room,
how it would have been

when they bought it—
in what? 1919, was it?

And how we long to buy
something here in this city.
Not a cottage,
but an apartment in Harlem
where we will dance,
my hand in yours,
the dogs growing excited
beneath our feet.
Where someday
someone might wonder
if this is how it was
when they lived here?

⚭

I meet you
in the street after work,
after another night at the sex club
where I talk to men about fucking
about risk,
about connection.
Where I test men
for HIV and syphilis,
where drops of blood
tell the future—or is it the past?
The present?
Or maybe all three at once?

And tonight, the city is quiet
or as quiet as New York gets at 1 AM
on a weekday.
The Freedom Tower looks propped
against the sky like a backdrop to a musical—
the summer rain from earlier
has left everything turned to steam—a dream.
A drunk homeless man
smiles at us, stumbles a bit,
then says, *Good morning from Europe.*

∞

On the subway, a boy—five—maybe six—
opens a blue lunchbox
containing one inflated medical glove:
a bloated hand,
which he uses to bop his mother,
the side of the train car,
his own head.

His mother's nails
are all gold and glitter.
She doesn't respond,
so he stops,
turns to watch a passing train
speed ahead of us,
or are we speeding past it?

It's always so hard to tell.

And just like that the store rebuilds,
restocks, reopens.
And we rise up from the dead.
Fill the aisles like before.
Clang our baskets together.
And start again.

Self-Portrait as Unconscious Man at Bathhouse

They stand over him.
Him face down.
Him naked.
Him half out of the door:
cot, light, lube inside.
They stand over him—the police—
and ask if anyone knows him.
His ID at the front—locked away.
One man says he was with him.
With him but doesn't know him.
A body next to a body
is only a certain kind of knowing.
And now that body has stopped moving.
Is half out of the door.
On the floor.
Face down.
The police stand over him.
Ask questions.
Need to get his ID from the front:
who is this man?
As if an ID can tell you that.
A man on the floor.
Face down.
Him naked.
Him not moving.
His back a smooth arch of white.
His hair patches of gray.
None of this tells them who he is.
Or why.
Or how.

A name is in a drawer at the front.
Checked in.
But it takes time.
And he doesn't move.
Half out of the door.
Face down.
On the floor.
They stand over him calling:
sir—sir—sir.

The Day Miss Cleo Died

It's Tuesday in New York. 2016.
And the summer has finally turned
the subway stations into hell like it
always does. It's the end of July
and bodies run slick with sweat.
But before the heat of the day—
before work this morning—I pulled
a card from my Tarot deck—the one
you bought me a month ago after
my sudden interest (or is it need?)
in finding something to hold on to.
They say your first set should be
gifted and so you did: the Golden
deck. It's not all magic and fortune
telling. It's an analytical tool.
It's a way to tell yourself the story
you already know. I'm not crazy
is what I mean. But that's my own
skepticism coming through. My own
need to classify—to explain—to make
sense of the world. And today it was
Judgment—the card I pulled. A card
about facing reality. Of accepting
one's fate, one's errors. Some see it
as making amends like AA or as being
ready to accept punishment whatever
the cost. It's an ending, but also
a beginning. And then later I see her
face glowing on my phone and the headline:

MISS CLEO IS DEAD

Suddenly I'm back in Indiana,
late at night, the late '90s, her voice
echoing through the TV: *Call me*
today, the cards never lie, darling.
And how I wanted answers even then:
the corn knee high, the windows open,
the lightning bugs blinking on and off
like the train signal now in New York
where I suck in the heat and wait.

Everyone Shares Something

like a photo of a face / but not their face / just a face
names are not important
but gender can be / if it fits
a mugshot / passed around
maybe because he's hot / or she's not
or maybe because / well just look / you'll see
you'll laugh / you'll get the joke

like an article / about a man
with impressive degrees / Ivy League schools
how he was denied / license to practice law
because he has a criminal / record
a reminder / that haunts you
that gets passed around / and around
not about you / but around you
never knowing you / could be him
without the fanciness / without the outrage
without the Ivy League

like when you finally check YouTube
after months of fear / better not to know
how you search for your face / in motion
how your body moved / that night
almost on its own / almost like magic
looking for the footage that loops / in your brain
that you see when you close / your eyes
but that's memory / not fact
not video / not on YouTube
nothing is there / to pass around / to share

This Isn't *Law & Order*

There's a list of names on the door
and a bucket of case files,
which a young representative
from the DA's office fishes through,
scratching her head,
trying to make sense of procedure,
of rules,
of lives scrawled onto pads
while the public defenders swim
through the pews calling out names
because they don't know clients by faces.
Luckily, I could afford my own
who knows my face for $2,500
(a bargain).

I wait my turn.
I watch an older woman take a plea deal,
hand over certificates for classes
she's taken online:
court-ordered classes
that are meant to teach her not to abuse
her patients at the nursing home
where she works—
where she still works
because she's in her uniform on her way to work.
I don't know if any online class
can teach you not to abuse people,
but either way
the courts will have these sheets of paper.
Documentation is important.

No, this is not a long-running TV program.
No one is getting gunned down
on the steps outside.
There are no cries from the crowd.
Just sighs and paperwork.
Sign here
and here
and here
and now you can go.
But your life's not the same.
You are a felon now.
You are a criminal.

Yes, take a deal.
Plea it out.
Save us money.
But confess, so we know you really mean it
and aren't doing it for another reason
like lack of time,
money,
or energy for a real defense.

And these faces aren't Hollywood types.
The defense attorneys aren't arrogant assholes
like they are on TV,
and the prosecutors are not all power and grace.
In fact, they're mostly fumbling
with folders,
glancing at details of cases they've barely seen.
No one knows your story.

There's no time for that.

But there is time for the judge to be late.
For the clerk to get coffee.
For the officers to laugh.
For the detective with the old man in handcuffs
in the front row to check Facebook
and watch makeup tutorials on YouTube.

And I wait,
wishing I could flip the channel,
wishing I had a surprise witness,
wishing I had Benson on my side,
wishing my whiteness or maleness or something
could save me like they always say it will.
But nothing comes.
Just sign here.
And here.
And here.

For the Devil Works in the Red That Spins Your Finger

At night, your hand, my hair: the weight of it spinning
        through the red, putting you to sleep
like a spell, like a forgotten power, like magic
        suddenly awake in my bones from long ago,
another life, another time, another story.
        Like Grimm's Iron Hans who was red all over:
beard and body. A rusty, wild man whose story
        was later used by the Men's Movement
(whatever that is) to say something about masculinity,
        but nothing about redness.

They say the devil is here in the red creeping
        from my roots. Like I never stood a chance:
Wicked comes this way. Only one to two percent
        of the population has red hair.
The rarest color. Like *Anne of Green Gables*, books
        I read with my mother years ago.
Her hair not red, but chemo-thin now from six months
        of treatment. But she is not here and her hair,
she says, is going to be okay and mine is longer now
        and redder and I own it: redhead, ginger boy,
matching drapes and carpet. And every few years the Internet
        explodes with myths of our extinction:
the dying gingers, the fading red, the end of days
        that is always approaching but never comes.

In Medieval times, red hair was the mark of the beast.
        The mark of sexual desire. The mark of moral
degeneration. The mark of a witch, a werewolf, a vampire.

Something to fear. Stories to tell at night
around fires burning bright. And years ago, my therapist
        in Florida, the one with the pug which he never
let me hold, which is the only reason I picked him,
        told me I was hypersexual, told me he could do
nothing for me, told me my expectations were unreasonable.
        I just wanted to hold his pug.

In the 19ᵗʰ century, records indicate 48% of women
        who committed crimes were redheads—
or were they just the ones accused? We are always guilty,
        aren't we? Kick a Ginger Day turned into
Kill a Ginger Day turned into Kiss a Ginger Day
        and on we spin. Thor, the god of thunder,
is described as having red hair. Take that Chris Hemsworth.
        In pop culture, redheads are often the loser
or the bully. Sometimes sexy, but only if you are female
        (Prince Harry excluded). But in real life it's all:
I love gingers. Does the carpet match the drapes? Can I see?
        I hear redheads are good in bed, is it true?
Show me. Love me. Fuck me.

Judas and Mary Magdalene are both depicted
        with red hair. Red that shocks the night.
Red that makes the narrative take shape—creates
        our expectations—our history.
Like a map suddenly laid out in the strands of red
        that spin your finger at night in bed—
you fast asleep—me wide awake.

Not Telling My Parents I'm a Convicted Felon While Visiting an Agnes Martin Exhibit at the Guggenheim

There are lines here—
thin lines,
graphite lines,
gray, black, blue,
white lines—
sometimes almost pink lines.
One painting looks like a lineup
marking heights like they always show
in movies or on television.
And there are shapes here
and there—
stark white,
just an outline,
a triangle,
a circle.
And we walk uphill.
It's all uphill.
A spiral.
And the farther we go
the more it makes sense:
the images,
the lines,
where they meet and where they don't,
and our relationship to distance:
how standing back creates
a different image than up close.
And they are enjoying themselves—
my parents—

older each time I see them—
surprising me with their comments
and insights
and interest in an artist
who doesn't just make "pretty pictures."
And in this bubble
nothing seems impossible—
nothing seems unspeakable.
But Martin focused on the positive emotions.
On happiness.
Are we happy?
My lawyer says when the charges
are lowered,
after my six months,
they will take my DNA—a state law.
A swab of my cheek kept on file.
He mentions matching cold cases
like a TV show.
My DNA:
a combination of my parents
held captive for all time
in a space less clear
than the grids before us
or the wash of gray lines
on her final painting
at the top of the museum
where we must turn around
and return to the beginning—
which is now the exit.

Proxy

To hold power or authority or agency for another. To hold their office or position or function. Sometimes temporarily. To give one's self over in ability—not fully in body—but sometimes like power of attorney or voting power. To be able to speak for another or maybe just speaking in a voice empowered by another's silence, which isn't the same.

∾

A proxy server is a server that works as a medium between other servers, taking requests for that server, evaluating and controlling those requests, and creating structure within the wider system of servers. Whatever that means.

∾

When my mother was diagnosed with leukemia, I wanted to send a proxy—someone to take on the role of comforter, of dutiful son, of healer. To be there and not there at the exact same time. To proxy myself. To relieve the guilt. To survive the unthinkable.

∾

A web proxy is a proxy that allows you to search the Internet anonymously, protecting your identity, your privacy, your fetishes. No one has to know you collect Barbie Doll shoes or look at cuckold porn or shop at Walmart when the deals are good. It hides everything.

∾

But what of the trick of the proxy? When you get someone to do what you want without them knowing you created the fate that will lead to the outcome you desire most? When you control the proxy without them knowing they are a proxy? When power is yours within the given system? What then?

∽

I search the Internet for articles about people who killed children, confessed, and were executed all to avoid the mortal sin of suicide in the 18th century. Men and women so caught in their own belief system they could not see the error of their ways. A suicide by proxy it is called. And no, I did not use a web proxy. I am exposed.

∽

Hindus believe in reincarnation. That after physical death, one can return to Earth in another form—another body—a proxy of sorts. Like a thin line that connects one body to another through time: a strand of hair, a looking glass, a page. The ability to be more than one person. To live many lives—make many mistakes—many regrets—to never be sure if this is the last time or the last one.

Conditional Discharge

It's yes, your honor
and no, your honor
and law-abiding promises
to take care of my family
and sheets of paper
never fully explained:
check boxes
and numbers
and codes that mean I did something wrong
but now after six months
let's call it something else:
a misdemeanor
but everything could change
if I step out of line
if I don't pay the court fees
if I don't get my mouth swabbed
(*rub it left and right and on my tongue like a lollipop*)
and if I don't get my index fingers pressed to ink
(real this time)
and if I don't lead a productive life
(whatever that means)
though no one here knows my life
or even my name
it's misspelled on all the sheets of paper
I tell them over and over
and all I get is a nod and a question:
but does it match the rest?
yes, all the papers match
yes, all the papers are wrong
yes, your honor

and no, your honor
and so I am discharged
conditionally
sent into the world
with poems in my pocket
from the Supreme Court
of the State of New York

Epilogue

I never wanted to die (like those other stories)
I never wanted to go to prison
(though it would've made for good material)

It's easy to convince yourself of almost anything:
a religion
(which I did away with long ago),
a planted memory
(told over and over until it becomes true),
or maybe something you read once
that you wished were true,
that you wished were you,
and then it was

I never wanted to die (that doesn't mean I won't)
I never wanted to go to prison
(so I signed and signed and signed)

Maybe they were right all along:
our greatest enemy is the black bile inside us

Or maybe it's our inability to learn from the past:
(red into red into red)
Everything fading into something else
Everything getting rewritten

Am I Mary?
Or just a mary?
Or is she me?

Notes

The poems in "Part I" are indebted to the research done by Professor Kathy Stuart. Her articles "Suicide by Proxy: the Unintended Consequences of Public Executions in Eighteenth-Century Germany" and "Melancholy Murderers: Suicide by Proxy and the Insanity Defense" greatly influenced my fictional telling of Mary Agnes' suicide by proxy. I first heard about this phenomenon when Stuart appeared on *This American Life* in 2012.

18th Century Melancholia: This poem opens with a line from Julie Marie Wade's poem "Layover" from her book *Six* (2016).

Land Is Something You Crave or You Don't: The title of this poem is taken from Nick Reding's book *Methland: The Death and Life of An American Small Town* (2009). The opening quote is from Bruce Snider's poem "Map" from his book *Paradise, Indiana* (2012).

By the Numbers: Statistics in this poem were taken from the Death Penalty Information Center at the time it was written.

You Don't Look Violent: This poem is dedicated to my friend Jaclyn.

Self-Portrait as a Danny Lyon Prison Photograph from 1968 at The Whitney: This poem is based on work by the photographer Danny Lyon at The Whitney's exhibit "Danny Lyon: Message to the Future" in Summer of 2016.

The Day Miss Cleo Died: This poem refers to the death of Miss Cleo (aka Youree Dell Harris, aka Rae Dell Harris or Cleomili Perris Youree or Ree Perris) of cancer on July 26, 2016. In the late '90s she became the face of a psychic hotline that was later at the center of a major fraud case. This piece also pays tribute to Frank O'Hara's famous poem "The Day Lady Died." The week of Miss Cleo's death also marked the 50th anniversary of Frank O'Hara's death.

Domestic Terror: "Rikers is Here" stickers were placed on subway maps around the city in the spring of 2016 as part of a social justice project by three graduate students (Estefanía Acosta de la Peña, Laura Sánchez, and Misha Volf) at The New School.

My Jesus Year: The fourth section of this poem refers to the Broadway musical *American Psycho*, which opened in spring of 2016 and refers particularly to the final song of the show "This is Not an Exit."

Not Telling My Parents I'm a Convicted Felon While Visiting an Agnes Martin Exhibit at the Guggenheim: This poem refers to the Agnes Martin exhibit at the Guggenheim that opened in October of 2016.

Other texts that influenced and informed this book include: *Hanging Between Heaven and Earth: Capital Crime, Execution Preaching, and Theology in Early New England* by Scott D. Seay (2009), *The Autobiography of an Execution* by David R. Dow (2010), and numerous articles about the U.S. justice system.

Acknowledgments

I'm grateful to the following journals where some of these poems previously appeared (sometimes in different versions):

Queen Mob's Tea House ("How We Became Sluts"); *Assaracus* ("My Husband Talks of Floating"); *Midwestern Gothic* ("The Day Miss Cleo Died"); *The Account* ("My Jesus Year"); *Impossible Archetype* ("Domestic Terror").

I'm continuously thankful to all the teachers in my life from those I've known personally to those I've only known through the page. Thank you to my publisher, Bryan Borland, who has believed in my work for so many years and has helped make my dreams come true. Gratitude to Seth Pennington for his hard work in creating this book.

Special love and appreciation to Jaclyn Sullivan Lauer for her insights, support, and friendship. And finally, to my husband, Dustin Carter, who has never stopped believing in me. Thank you.

About the Poet

Stephen S. Mills is the author of the Lambda Award-winning book *He Do the Gay Man in Different Voices* and *A History of the Unmarried,* both from Sibling Rivalry Press. He earned his MFA from Florida State University and is winner of both the 2008 Gival Press Oscar Wilde Poetry Award and the 2014 Christopher Hewitt Award for Fiction. He lives in New York with his husband, Dustin Carter, and two schnauzers. For more, visit www.stephensmills.com.

About the Press

Sibling Rivalry Press is an independent press based in Little Rock, Arkansas. It is a sponsored project of Fractured Atlas, a nonprofit arts service organization. Contributions to support the operations of Sibling Rivalry Press are tax-deductible to the extent permitted by law, and your donations will directly assist in the publication of work that disturbs and enraptures. To contribute to the publication of more books like this one, please visit our website and click *donate*.

Sibling Rivalry Press gratefully acknowledges the following donors, without whom this book would not be possible:

Liz Ahl	Bill La Civita
Stephanie Anderson	Mollie Lacy
Priscilla Atkins	Anthony Lioi
John Bateman	Catherine Lundoff
Sally Bellerose & Cynthia Suopis	Adrian M.
Jen Benka	Ed Madden
Dustin Brookshire	Open Mouth Reading Series
Sarah Browning	Red Hen Press
Russell Bunge	Steven Reigns
Michelle Castleberry	Paul Romero
Don Cellini	Erik Schuckers
Philip F. Clark	Alana Smoot
Risa Denenberg	Stillhouse Press
Alex Gildzen	KMA Sullivan
J. Andrew Goodman	Billie Swift
Sara Gregory	Tony Taylor
Karen Hayes	Hugh Tipping
Wayne B. Johnson & Marcos L. Martínez	Eric Tran
Jessica Manack	Ursus Americanus Press
Alicia Mountain	Julie Marie Wade
Rob Jacques	Ray Warman & Dan Kiser
Nahal Suzanne Jamir	Anonymous (14)